So Much Nonsense

Edward Lear

with an introduction by

Quentin Blake

Bodleian Library
UNIVERSITY OF OXFORD

This edition first published in 2007 by the Bodleian Library,
Broad Street, Oxford OX1 3BG

www.bodleianbookshop.co.uk

ISBN   1 85124 390 9
ISBN 13   978 1 85124 390 7

Original material first published in the following volumes by Edward Lear:
pp. 1–3 from *Nonsense Songs, Stories, Botany and Alphabets*, 1871;
pp. 4–113, 214 from *A Book of Nonsense*, 1846;
pp. 114–213, 215–40 from *More Nonsense Pictures, Rhymes, Botany, etc.*, 1872;
pp. 241–7 from *Nonsense Songs and Stories*, 1895.

The drawings on pp. i and 248 are from a letter by Edward Lear inscribed
'Corfu. June 4 [1863]', now in the Dunston Collection, Bodleian Library.

Quotation in introduction taken from *Edward Lear: The Life of a Wanderer*
by Vivien Noakes. Reproduced by kind permission of Sutton Publishing.

Designed by Dot Little. Layout by illuminati, Grosmont.
Printed and bound by South Sea International Press, China.

British Library Catalogue in Publishing Data
A CIP record of this publication is available from the British Library

Introduction

Perhaps we can never quite revive the sense of surprise that must have attended the appearance of Edward Lear's *Nonsense Verses*, any more than we can for that other distinctively Victorian phenomenon, the Gilbert *&* Sullivan operas. Nevertheless if you haven't seen Lear's drawings for the verses—or haven't seen them recently—there is still, I think, an element of surprise about them. Even though we have long lost the nineteenth-century sense of visual proprieties, we can still feel that there are conventions that are vigorously being wrested out of shape.

The indulgence allowed to Lear at that time—the permission to be playful—was of course because these drawings and verses were for *children*. Even so they must have been in striking contrast to the cross-hatched formality of most of the illustrations considered appropriate for the young reader. But then these were produced, verses and drawings together, pretty well impromptu, not originally for publication but for the entertainment of a specific young audience.

They were the children of Knowsley Hall, seat of the octogenarian Lord Stanley, although Edward Lear did not find himself there for the entertainment of these children. The great house boasted room not only for a whole tribe of family and guests, but for a menagerie of wild creatures too, and so this gifted young artist—already celebrated for his parrot illustrations, though barely twenty—was employed to depict them.

In a sense nothing could be further from the magnificent felicities of Lear's natural history work than these crazy, intense little spontaneities; yet they were also the work of an artist. If we look at those later drawings and watercolours which were the fruit of Lear's wanderings around the Mediterranean, we encounter, in very different circumstances, the same slow-motion, slashing pen-stroke: living, alert, controlled. The nonsense drawings have a sort of graphic authority, and in their economy Lear anticipated what many years later became the shorthand language of the cartoonist. The fact that they are fundamentally professional is one of the points touched on in a characterisation of the nonsense drawings that Vivien Noakes includes in her biography of Lear, which is hardly to be improved upon:

> Children's book illustrations then were generally either rather stilted woodcuts, or elaborate, often very charming, drawings—but the illustrations to the limericks are fresh and clear and almost crude in their simplicity, yet at the same time they are very professional.
>
> Running through them all is a sense of movement—the arms are flung spontaneously back like birds in flight and the legs stride out or stand poised expectantly on tip-toe as if they are going to be

spun round like a child's top. There is none of the genteel decorum which was thought so proper but instead, like children, the Old Men and Women are hardly ever still and nobody minds at all.

The nonsense drawings and their verses go so well and naturally together that hardly anybody has felt the necessity of commenting on it. The verses in fact seem to have been an adaptation of an existing limerick form of the time.

> There was a sick man of Tobago
> Liv'd long on rice-gruel and sago
> But at last, to his bliss,
> The physician said this—
> 'To a roast leg of mutton you may go.'

It's easy to see in this the slightly hard-working humour typical of the early issues of *Punch* of the mid-century: something which disappears completely when Lear switches into a parallel world of extraordinariness. The name of the place prompts the rhyme, however unlikely it may seem, so that nonsense is always waiting in the wings. The Young Lady of Corsica is destined to purchase a little brown saucy-cur as the Old Person of Putney was destined to eat roast spiders and chutney, and the Old Man of Whitehaven to dance a quadrille with a Raven. It's Lear's own quirks of fancy, of course, that supply the roast spiders and the quadrille, and another rather different one that gives us that final line 'so they smashed that Old Man of Whitehaven'.

It is this note of ruthlessness that was later taken up and exploited by Belloc in *his* verses for children. It's a note that, at any rate in my view, one is grateful for in Lear, in contrast to the occasional over-amiable whimsy from the pen of a 'Derry-down-Derry who loves to make little folks merry.'

No doubt Kingsley Amis, who didn't find it hard to look down on any form of humour that didn't chime with his own, would agree with this; more particularly, I seem to remember, he took Lear to task for the fact that the last line of his verse often very nearly matches the first. It's true that it is normally the business of a limerick to provide a surprise at this point, clinched by the rhyme. Lear doesn't do this, but although his way risks bathos, what it does do is to shunt our attention back on the situation (and its verbal adornments). 'That *ecstatic* Old Person of Tring'; 'That *expensive* Young Lady of Corsica'.

And they are situations that are constantly (a blessing for the artist–illustrator) *giving Lear something to draw*. How he embraced the opportunity! The conviction of the drawings seems to impress on us that these things are true, at any rate in this parallel nonsense world. Lear displayed many characteristics that we can think of as of his time: energy, melancholia, a longing for the elsewhere of solitary travel, an ear for Tennysonian cadences. But equally the eccentricity of his humour and the fierceness of his drawing hand gave him, in his own strange way, entry into ours.

Quentin Blake

THE OWL AND THE PUSSY-CAT

I

The Owl and the Pussy-cat went to sea
    In a beautiful pea-green boat,
They took some honey, and plenty of money,
    Wrapped up in a five-pound note.
The Owl looked up to the stars above,
    And sang to a small guitar,
'O lovely Pussy! O Pussy, my love,
    What a beautiful Pussy you are,
        You are,
        You are!
What a beautiful Pussy you are!'

II

Pussy said to the Owl, 'You elegant fowl!
　　How charmingly sweet you sing!
O let us be married! too long we have tarried:
　　But what shall we do for a ring?'
They sailed away, for a year and a day,
　　To the land where the Bong-tree grows
And there in a wood a Piggy-wig stood
　　With a ring at the end of his nose,
　　　　His nose,
　　　　His nose,
With a ring at the end of his nose.

III

'Dear Pig, are you willing to sell for one shilling
    Your ring?' Said the Piggy, 'I will.'
So they took it away, and were married next day
    By the Turkey who lives on the hill.
They dined on mince, and slices of quince,
    Which they ate with a runcible spoon;

And hand in hand, on the edge of the sand,
    They danced by the light of the moon,
        The moon,
        The moon,
They danced by the light of the moon.

NONSENSE VERSE

There was an Old Man with a beard,
Who said, 'It is just as I feared!—
Two Owls and a Hen, four Larks and a Wren,
Have all built their nests in my beard!'

There was a Young Lady of Ryde,
Whose shoe-strings were seldom untied;
She purchased some clogs, and some small spotty dogs,
And frequently walked about Ryde.

There was an Old Man with a nose,
Who said, 'If you choose to suppose,
That my nose is too long, you are certainly wrong!'
That remarkable Man with a nose.

There was an Old Man on a hill,
Who seldom, if ever, stood still;
He ran up and down, in his Grandmother's gown,
Which adorned that Old Man on a hill.

There was a Young Lady whose bonnet,
Came untied when the birds sate upon it;
But she said, 'I don't care! All the birds in the air
Are welcome to sit on my bonnet!'

There was a Young Person of Smyrna,
Whose Grandmother threatened to burn her;
But she seized on the Cat, and said, 'Granny, burn that!
You incongruous Old Woman of Smyrna!'

There was an Old Person of Chili,
Whose conduct was painful and silly,
He sate on the stairs, eating apples and pears,
That imprudent Old Person of Chili.

There was an Old Man with a gong,
Who bumped at it all the day long;
But they called out, 'O law! you're a horrid old bore!'
So they smashed that Old Man with a gong.

There was an Old Lady of Chertsey,
Who made a remarkable curtsey;
She twirled round and round, till she sunk underground,
Which distressed all the people of Chertsey.

There was an Old Man in a tree,
Who was horribly bored by a Bee;
When they said, 'Does it buzz?' he replied, 'Yes, it does!'
'It's a regular brute of a Bee!'

There was an Old Man with a flute,
A sarpint ran into his boot;
But he played day and night, till the sarpint took flight,
And avoided that Man with a flute.

There was a Young Lady whose chin,
Resembled the point of a pin;
So she had it made sharp, and purchased a harp,
And played several tunes with her chin.

There was an Old Man of Kilkenny,
Who never had more than a penny;
He spent all that money, in onions and honey,
That wayward Old Man of Kilkenny.

There was an Old Person of Ischia,
Whose conduct grew friskier and friskier;
He danced hornpipes and jigs, and ate thousands of figs,
That lively Old Person of Ischia.

There was an Old Man in a boat,
Who said, 'I'm afloat! I'm afloat!'
When they said, 'No! you ain't!' he was ready to faint,
That unhappy Old Man in a boat.

There was a Young Lady of Portugal,
Whose ideas were excessively nautical:
She climbed up a tree, to examine the sea,
But declared she would never leave Portugal.

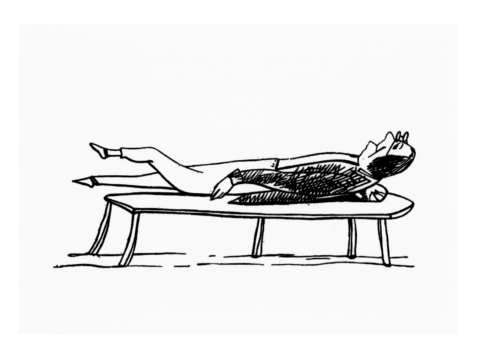

There was an Old Man of Moldavia,
Who had the most curious behaviour;
For while he was able, he slept on a table.
That funny Old Man of Moldavia.

There was an Old Man of Madras,
Who rode on a cream-coloured ass;
But the length of its ears, so promoted his fears,
That it killed that Old Man of Madras,

There was an Old Person of Leeds,
Whose head was infested with beads;
She sat on a stool, and ate gooseberry fool,
Which agreed with that Person of Leeds.

There was an Old Man of Peru,
Who never knew what he should do;
So he tore off his hair, and behaved like a bear,
That intrinsic Old Man of Peru.

There was an Old Person of Hurst,
Who drank when he was not athirst;
When they said, 'You'll grow fatter' he answered,
   'What matter?'
That globular Person of Hurst.

There was a Young Person of Crete,
Whose toilette was far from complete;
She dressed in a sack, spickle-speckled with black,
That ombliferous Person of Crete.

There was an Old Man of the Isles,
Whose face was pervaded with smiles:
He sung high dum diddle, and played on the fiddle,
That amiable Man of the Isles.

There was an Old Person of Buda,
Whose conduct grew ruder and ruder;
Till at last, with a hammer, they silenced his clamour,
By smashing that Person of Buda.

There was an Old Man of Columbia,
Who was thirsty, and called out for some beer;
But they brought it quite hot, in a small copper pot,
Which disgusted that Man of Columbia.

There was a Young Lady of Dorking,
Who bought a large bonnet for walking;
But its colour and size, so bedazzled her eyes,
That she very soon went back to Dorking.

There was an Old Man who supposed,
That the street door was partially closed;
But some very large rats, ate his coats and his hats,
While that futile Old Gentleman dozed.

There was an Old Man of the West,
Who wore a pale plum-coloured vest;
When they said, 'Does it fit?' he replied, 'Not a bit!'
That uneasy Old Man of the West.

There was an Old Man of the Wrekin
Whose shoes made a horrible creaking
But they said 'Tell us whether, your shoes are of leather,
Or of what, you Old Man of the Wrekin?'

There was a Young Lady whose eyes,
Were unique as to colour and size;
When she opened them wide, people all turned aside,
And started away in surprise.

There was a Young Lady of Norway,
Who casually sat in a doorway;
When the door squeezed her flat, she exclaimed
    'What of that?'
This courageous Young Lady of Norway.

There was an Old Man of Vienna,
Who lived upon Tincture of Senna;
When that did not agree, he took Camomile Tea,
That nasty Old Man of Vienna.

There was an Old Person whose habits,
Induced him to feed upon Rabbits;
When he'd eaten eighteen, he turned perfectly green,
Upon which he relinquished those habits.

There was an Old Person of Dover,
Who rushed through a field of blue Clover;
But some very large bees, stung his nose and his knees,
So he very soon went back to Dover.

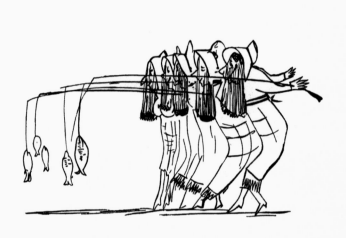

There was an Old Man of Marseilles,
Whose daughters wore bottle-green veils;
They caught several Fish, which they put in a dish,
And sent to their Pa' at Marseilles.

There was an Old Person of Cadiz,
Who was always polite to all ladies;
But in handing his daughter, he fell into the water,
Which drowned that Old Person of Cadiz.

There was an Old Person of Basing,
Whose presence of mind was amazing;
He purchased a steed, which he rode at full speed,
And escaped from the people of Basing.

There was an Old Man of Quebec,
A beetle ran over his neck;
But he cried, 'With a needle, I'll slay you, O beadle!'
That angry Old Man of Quebec.

There was an Old Person of Philœ,
Whose conduct was scroobious and wily;
He rushed up a Palm, when the weather was calm,
And observed all the ruins of Philœ.

There was a Young Lady of Bute,
Who played on a silver-gilt flute;
She played several jigs, to her uncle's white pigs,
That amusing Young Lady of Bute.

There was a Young Lady whose nose,
Was so long that it reached to her toes;
So she hired an Old Lady, whose conduct was steady,
To carry that wonderful nose.

There was a Young Lady of Turkey,
Who wept when the weather was murky;
When the day turned out fine, she ceased to repine,
That capricious Young Lady of Turkey.

There was an Old Man of Apulia,
Whose conduct was very peculiar
He fed twenty sons, upon nothing but buns,
That whimsical Man of Apulia.

There was an Old Man with a poker,
Who painted his face with red oker
When they said, 'You're a Guy!' he made no reply,
But knocked them all down with his poker.

There was an Old Person of Prague,
Who was suddenly seized with the plague;
But they gave him some butter, which caused him
    to mutter,
And cured that Old Person of Prague.

There was an Old Man of the North,
Who fell into a basin of broth;
But a laudable cook, fished him out with a hook,
Which saved that Old Man of the North.

There was a Young Lady of Poole,
Whose soup was excessively cool;
So she put it to boil by the aid of some oil,
That ingenious Young Lady of Poole.

There was an Old Person of Mold,
Who shrank from sensations of cold;
So he purchased some muffs, some furs and some fluffs,
And wrapped himself from the cold.

There was an Old Man of Nepaul,
From his horse had a terrible fall;
But, though split quite in two, by some very strong glue,
They mended that Man of Nepaul.

There was an old Man of th' Abruzzi,
So blind that he couldn't his foot see;
When they said, 'That's your toe,' he replied, 'Is it so?'
That doubtful old Man of th' Abruzzi.

There was an Old Person of Rhodes,
Who strongly objected to toads;
He paid several cousins, to catch them by dozens,
That futile Old Person of Rhodes.

There was an Old Man of Peru,
Who watched his wife making a stew;
But once by mistake, in a stove she did bake,
That unfortunate Man of Peru.

There was an Old Man of Melrose,
Who walked on the tips of his toes;
But they said, 'It ain't pleasant, to see you at present,
You stupid Old Man of Melrose.'

There was a Young Lady of Lucca,
Whose lovers completely forsook her;
She ran up a tree, and said, 'Fiddle-de-dee!'
Which embarassed the people of Lucca.

There was an Old Man of Bohemia,
Whose daughter was christened Euphemia;
Till one day, to his grief, she married a thief,
Which grieved that Old Man of Bohemia.

There was an Old Man of Vesuvius,
Who studied the works of Vitruvius;
When the flames burnt his book, to drinking he took,
That morbid Old Man of Vesuvius.

There was an Old Man of Cape Horn,
Who wished he had never been born;
So he sat on a chair, till he died of despair,
That dolorous Man of Cape Horn.

There was an Old Lady whose folly,
Induced her to sit in a holly;
Whereon by a thorn, her dress being torn,
She quickly became melancholy.

There was an Old Man of Corfu,
Who never knew what he should do;
So he rushed up and down, till the sun made him brown,
That bewildered Old Man of Corfu.

There was an Old Man of the South,
Who had an immoderate mouth;
But in swallowing a dish, that was quite full of fish,
He was choked, that Old Man of the South.

There was an Old Man of the Nile,
Who sharpened his nails with a file;
Till he cut off his thumbs, and said calmly, 'This comes—
Of sharpening one's nails with a file!'

There was an Old Person of Rheims,
Who was troubled with horrible dreams;
So, to keep him awake, they fed him with cake.
Which amused that Old Person of Rheims.

There was an Old Person of Cromer,
Who stood on one leg to read Homer;
When he found he grew stiff, he jumped over the cliff,
Which concluded that Person of Cromer.

There was an Old Person of Troy,
Whose drink was warm brandy and soy;
Which he took with a spoon, by the light of the moon,
In sight of the city of Troy.

There was an Old Man of the Dee,
Who was sadly annoyed by a flea;
When he said, 'I will scratch it'—they gave him a hatchet,
Which grieved that Old Man of the Dee.

There was an Old Man of Dundee,
Who frequented the top of a tree;
When disturbed by the crows, he abruptly arose,
And exclaimed, 'I'll return to Dundee.'

There was an Old Person of Tring,
Who embellished his nose with a ring;
He gazed at the moon, every evening in June,
That ecstatic Old Person of Tring.

There was an Old Man on some rocks,

Who shut his wife up in a box,

When she said, 'Let me out,' he exclaimed, 'Without
doubt,

You will pass all your life in that box.'

There was an Old Man of Coblenz,
The length of whose legs was immense;
He went with one prance, from Turkey to France,
That surprising Old Man of Coblenz.

There was an Old Man of Calcutta,
Who perpetually ate bread and butter;
Till a great bit of muffin, on which he was stuffing,
Choked that horrid Old Man of Calcutta.

There was an Old Man in a pew,
Whose waistcoat was spotted with blue;
But he tore it in pieces, to give to his nieces,
That cheerful Old Man in a pew.

There was an Old Man who said,
'How—shall I flee from this horrible Cow?
I will sit on this stile, and continue to smile,
Which may soften the heart of that Cow.'

There was a Young Lady of Hull,
Who was chased by a virulent Bull;
But she seized on a spade, and called out—'Who's afraid!'
Which distracted that virulent Bull.

There was an Old Man of Whitehaven,
Who danced a quadrille with a Raven;
But they said—'It's absurd, to encourage this bird!'
So they smashed that Old Man of Whitehaven.

There was an Old Man of Leghorn,
The smallest as ever was born;
But quickly snapt up he, was once by a puppy,
Who devoured that Old Man of Leghorn.

There was an Old Man of the Hague,
Whose ideas were excessively vague;
He built a balloon, to examine the moon,
That deluded Old Man of the Hague.

There was a Young Lady of Tyre,
Who swept the loud chords of a lyre;
At the sound of each sweep, she enraptured the deep,
And enchanted the city of Tyre.

There was an Old Man who said, 'Hush!
I perceive a young bird in this bush!'
When they said—'Is it small?' he replied—'Not at all!
It is four times as big as the bush!'

There was an Old Man of the East,
Who gave all his children a feast;
But they all eat so much, and their conduct was such,
That it killed that Old Man of the East.

There was an Old Man of Kamschatka,
Who possessed a remarkably fat cur.
His gait and his waddle, were held as a model,
To all the fat dogs in Kamschatka.

There was an Old Man of the Coast,
Who placidly sat on a post;
But when it was cold, he relinquished his hold,
And called for some hot buttered toast.

There was an Old Person of Bangor,
Whose face was distorted with anger,
He tore off his boots, and subsisted on roots,
That borascible Person of Bangor.

There was an Old Man with a beard,
Who sat on a horse when he reared;
But they said, 'Never mind! you will fall off behind,
You propitious Old Man with a beard!'

There was an Old Man of the West,
Who never could get any rest;
So they set him to spin, on his nose and his chin,
Which cured that Old Man of the West.

There was an Old Person of Anerley,
Whose conduct was strange and unmannerly;
He rushed down the Strand, with a Pig in each hand,
But returned in the evening to Anerley.

There was a Young Lady of Troy,
Whom several large flies did annoy;
Some she killed with a thump, some she drowned
　　at the pump,
And some she took with her to Troy.

There was an Old Man of Berlin,
Whose form was uncommonly thin;
Till he once, by mistake, was mixed up in a cake,
So they baked that Old Man of Berlin.

There was an Old Person of Spain,
Who hated all trouble and pain;
So he sate on a chair, with his feet in the air,
That umbrageous Old Person of Spain.

There was a Young Lady of Russia,
Who screamed so that no one could hush her;
Her screams were extreme, no one heard such a scream,
As was screamed by that Lady of Russia.

There was an Old Man who said, 'Well!
Will *nobody* answer this bell?
I have pulled day and night, till my hair has grown white,
But nobody answers this bell!'

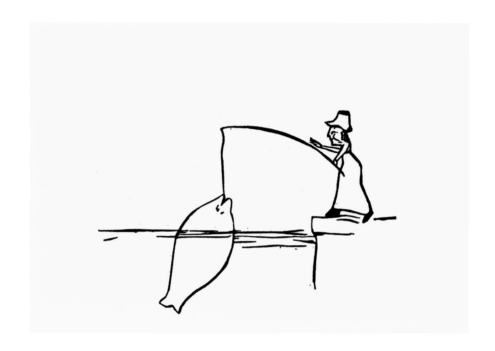

There was a Young Lady of Wales,
Who caught a large fish without scales;
When she lifted her hook, she exclaimed, 'Only look!'
That extatic Young Lady of Wales.

There was an Old Person of Cheadle,
Was put in the stocks by the beadle;
For stealing some pigs, some coats and some wigs,
That horrible Person of Cheadle.

There was a Young Lady of Welling,
Whose praise all the world was a telling;
She played on the harp, and caught several carp,
That accomplished Young Lady of Welling.

There was an Old Person of Tartary,
Who divided his jugular artery;
But he screeched to his wife, and she said, 'Oh, my life!
Your death will be felt by all Tartary!'

There was an Old Person of Chester,
Whom several small children did pester;
They threw some large stones, which broke most
    of his bones,
And displeased that Old Person of Chester.

There was an Old Man with an owl,
Who continued to bother and howl;
He sate on a rail, and imbibed bitter ale,
Which refreshed that Old Man and his owl.

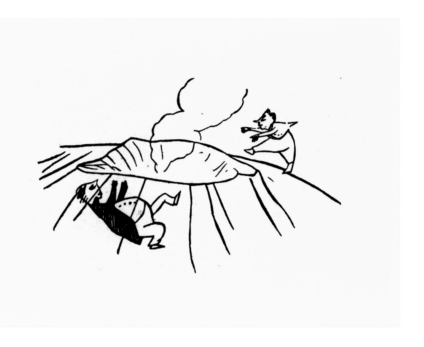

There was an Old Person of Gretna,
Who rushed down the crater of Etna;
When they said, 'Is it hot?' he replied, 'No, it's not!'
That mendacious Old Person of Gretna.

There was a Young Lady of Sweden,
Who went by the slow train to Weedon;
When they cried, 'Weedon Station!' she made no
    observation,
But she thought she should go back to Sweden.

There was a Young Girl of Majorca,
Whose aunt was a very fast walker;
She walked seventy miles, and leaped fifteen stiles,
Which astonished that Girl of Majorca.

There was an Old Man of the Cape,
Who possessed a large Barbary Ape;
Till the Ape one dark night, set the house on a light,
Which burned that Old Man of the Cape.

There was an Old Lady of Prague,
Whose language was horribly vague.
When they said, 'Are these caps?' she answered, 'Perhaps!'
That oracular Lady of Prague.

There was an Old Person of Sparta,
Who had twenty-five sons and one daughter;
He fed them on snails, and weighed them in scales,
That wonderful Person of Sparta.

There was an Old Man at a casement,
Who held up his hands in amazement;
When they said, 'Sir! You'll fall!' he replied, 'Not at all!'
That incipient Old Man at a casement.

There was an Old Person of Burton,
Whose answers were rather uncertain;
When they said, 'How d'ye do?' he replied, 'Who are you?'
That distressing Old Person of Burton.

There was an Old Person of Ems,
Who casually fell in the Thames;
And when he was found, they said he was drowned,
That unlucky Old Person of Ems.

There was an Old Person of Ewell,
Who chiefly subsisted on gruel;
But to make it more nice, he inserted some mice,
Which refreshed that Old Person of Ewell.

There was a Young Lady of Parma,
Whose conduct grew calmer and calmer;
When they said, 'Are you dumb?' she merely said, 'Hum!'
That provoking Young Lady of Parma.

There was an Old Man of Aôsta,
Who possessed a large Cow, but he lost her;
But they said, 'Don't you see, she has rushed up a tree?
You invidious Old Man of Aôsta!'

There was an Old Man, on whose nose,
Most birds of the air could repose;
But they all flew away, at the closing of day,
Which relieved that Old Man and his nose.

There was a Young Lady of Clare,
Who was sadly pursued by a bear;
When she found she was tired, she abruptly expired,
That unfortunate Lady of Clare.

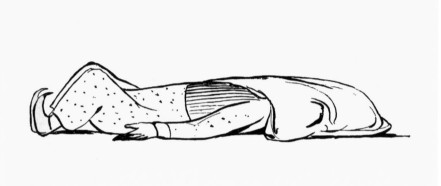

There was an Old Man of Hong Kong,
Who never did anything wrong;
He lay on his back, with his head in a sack,
That innocuous Old Man of Hong Kong.

There was an Old Person of Fife,
Who was greatly disgusted with life;
They sang him a ballad, and fed him on salad,
Which cured that Old Person of Fife.

There was a Young Person in green,
Who seldom was fit to be seen;
She wore a long shawl, over bonnet and all,
Which enveloped that Person in green.

There was an Old Person of Slough,
Who danced at the end of a bough;
But they said, 'If you sneeze, you might damage the trees,
You imprudent Old Person of Slough.'

There was an Old Person of Putney,
Whose food was roast spiders and chutney,
Which he took with his tea, within sight of the sea,
That romantic Old Person of Putney.

There was a Young Lady in white,
Who looked out at the depths of the night;
But the birds of the air, filled her heart with despair,
And oppressed that Young Lady in white.

There was an Old Person of Brill,
Who purchased a shirt with a frill;
But they said, 'Don't you wish, you may'nt look like a fish,
You obsequious Old Person of Brill?'

There was an Old Man of Three Bridges,
Whose mind was distracted by midges,
He sate on a wheel, eating underdone veal,
Which relieved that Old Man of Three Bridges.

There was an Old Person of Wick,
Who said, 'Tick-a-Tick, Tick-a-Tick;
Chickabee, Chickabaw,' And he said nothing more,
That laconic Old Person of Wick.

There was a Young Lady in blue,
Who said, 'Is it you? Is it you?'
When they said, 'Yes, it is,'—she replied only, 'Whizz!'
That ungracious Young Lady in blue.

There was an Old Person of China,
Whose daughters were Jiska and Dinah,
Amelia and Fluffy, Olivia and Chuffy,
And all of them settled in China.

There was an Old Man of the Dargle
Who purchased six barrels of Gargle;
For he said, 'I'll sit still, and will roll them down hill,
For the fish in the depths of the Dargle.'

There was an Old Man in a Marsh,
Whose manners were futile and harsh;
He sate on a log, and sang songs to a frog,
That instructive Old Man in a Marsh.

There was a Young Person in red,
Who carefully covered her head,
With a bonnet of leather, and three lines of feather,
Besides some long ribands of red.

There was an Old Person of Bree,
Who frequented the depths of the sea;
She nurs'd the small fishes, and washed all the dishes,
And swam back again into Bree.

There was an Old Man in a barge,
Whose nose was exceedingly large;
But in fishing by night, it supported a light,
Which helped that Old Man in a barge.

There was an Old Person in black,
A Grasshopper jumped on his back;
When it chirped in his ear, he was smitten with fear,
That helpless Old Person in black.

There was an Old Man of Toulouse
Who purchased a new pair of shoes;
When they asked, 'Are they pleasant?'—he said,
'Not at present!'
That turbid Old Man of Toulouse.

There was an Old Man of Blackheath,
Whose head was adorned with a wreath,
Of lobsters and spice, pickled onions and mice,
That uncommon Old Man of Blackheath.

There was an Old Man on the Humber,
Who dined on a cake of burnt Umber;
When he said—'It's enough!'—they only said, 'Stuff!
You amazing Old Man on the Humber!'

There was an Old Person of Stroud,
Who was horribly jammed in a crowd;
Some she slew with a kick, some she scrunched
   with a stick,
That impulsive Old Person of Stroud.

There was an Old Man of Boulak,
Who sate on a Crocodile's back;
But they said, 'Tow'rds the night, he may probably bite,
Which might vex you, Old Man of Boulak!'

There was an Old Man of Ibreem,
Who suddenly threaten'd to scream:
But they said, 'If you do, we will thump you quite blue,
You disgusting Old Man of Ibreem!'

There was an Old Lady of France,
Who taught little ducklings to dance;
When she said, 'Tick-a-tack!'—they only said, 'Quack!'
Which grieved that Old Lady of France.

There was an Old Man who screamed out
Whenever they knocked him about;
So they took off his boots, and fed him with fruits,
And continued to knock him about.

There was an Old Person of Woking,
Whose mind was perverse and provoking;
He sate on a rail, with his head in a pail,
That illusive Old Person of Woking.

There was a Young Person of Bantry,
Who frequently slept in the pantry;
When disturbed by the mice, she appeased them with rice
That judicious Young Person of Bantry.

There was an Old Man at a Junction,
Whose feelings were wrung with compunction,
When they said 'The Train's gone!' he exclaimed
    'How forlorn!'
But remained on the rails of the Junction.

There was an Old Man, who when little
Fell casually into a kettle;
But, growing too stout, he could never get out,
So he passed all his life in that kettle.

There was an Old Lady of Winchelsea,
Who said, 'If you needle or pin shall see,
On the floor of my room, sweep it up with the broom!'
That exhaustive Old Lady of Winchelsea!

There was a Young Lady of Firle,
Whose hair was addicted to curl;
It curled up a tree, and all over the sea,
That expansive Young Lady of Firle.

There was an Old Person of Rye,
Who went up to town on a fly;
But they said, 'If you cough, you are safe to fall off!
You abstemious Old Person of Rye!'

There was an Old Man of Messina,
Whose daughter was named Opsibeena;
She wore a small wig, and rode out on a pig,
To the perfect delight of Messina.

There is a Young Lady, whose nose,
Continually prospers and grows;
When it grew out of sight, she exclaimed in a fright,
'Oh! Farewell to the end of my nose!'

There was an Old Person of Cannes,
Who purchased three fowls and a fan;
Those she placed on a stool, and to make them feel cool
She constantly fanned them at Cannes.

There was an Old Person of Barnes,
Whose garments were covered with darns;
But they said, 'Without doubt, you will soon wear
   them out,
You luminous Person of Barnes!'

There was an Old Man of Cashmere,
Whose movements were scroobious and queer;
Being slender and tall, he looked over a wall,
And perceived two fat ducks of Cashmere.

There was an Old Person of Hove,
Who frequented the depths of a grove;
Where he studied his books, with the wrens and the rooks,
That tranquil Old Person of Hove.

There was an Old Person of Down,
Whose face was adorned with a frown;
When he opened the door, for one minute or more,
He alarmed all the people of Down.

There was an Old Man of Dunluce,
Who went out to sea on a goose:
When he'd gone out a mile, he observ'd with a smile,
'It is time to return to Dunluce.'

There was a Young Person of Kew,
Whose virtues and vices were few;
But with blameable haste, she devoured some hot paste,
Which destroyed that Young Person of Kew.

There was an Old Person of Sark,
Who made an unpleasant remark;
But they said, 'Don't you see what a brute you must be!'
You obnoxious Old Person of Sark.

There was an Old Person of Filey,
Of whom his acquaintance spoke highly;
He danced perfectly well, to the sound of a bell,
And delighted the people of Filey.

There was an Old Man of El Hums,
Who lived upon nothing but crumbs,
Which he picked off the ground, with the other birds
    round,
In the roads and the lanes of El Hums.

There was an Old Man of West Dumpet,
Who possessed a large nose like a trumpet;
When he blew it aloud, it astonished the crowd,
And was heard through the whole of West Dumpet.

There was an Old Man of Port Grigor,
Whose actions were noted for vigour;
He stood on his head, till his waistcoat turned red,
That eclectic Old Man of Port Grigor.

There was an Old Person of Bar,
Who passed all her life in a jar,
Which she painted pea-green, to appear more serene,
That placid Old Person of Bar.

There was an Old Person of Pett,
Who was partly consumed by regret;
He sate in a cart, and ate cold apple tart,
Which relieved that Old Person of Pett.

There was an Old Person of Newry,
Whose manners were tinctured with fury;
He tore all the rugs, and broke all the jugs
Within twenty miles' distance of Newry.

There was an Old Person of Jodd,
Whose ways were perplexing and odd;
She purchased a whistle, and sate on a thistle,
And squeaked to the people of Jodd.

There was an Old Person of Shoreham,
Whose habits were marked by decorum;
He bought an Umbrella, and sate in the cellar,
Which pleased all the people of Shoreham.

There was an Old Man of Dumbree,
Who taught little owls to drink tea;
For he said, 'To eat mice, is not proper or nice,'
That amiable Man of Dumbree.

There was an Old Person of Wilts,
Who constantly walked upon stilts;
He wreathed them with lilies, and daffy-down-dillies,
That elegant Person of Wilts.

There was an Old Man whose remorse,
Induced him to drink Caper Sauce;
For they said, 'If mixed up, with some cold claret-cup,
It will certainly soothe your remorse!'

There was an Old Person of Cassel,
Whose nose finished off in a tassel;
But they call'd out, 'Oh well!—don't it look like a bell!'
Which perplexed that Old Person of Cassel.

There was a Young Person of Janina,
Whose uncle was always a fanning her;
When he fanned off her head, she smiled sweetly,
    and said,
'You propitious Old Person of Janina!'

There was an Old Person of Ware,
Who rode on the back of a bear:
When they ask'd,—'Does it trot?'—he said
   'Certainly not!
He's a Moppsikon Floppsikon bear!'

There was an Old Person of Dean
Who dined on one pea, and one bean;
For he said, 'More than that, would make me too fat,'
That cautious Old Person of Dean.

There was an Old Person of Dundalk,
Who tried to teach fishes to walk;
When they tumbled down dead, he grew weary, and said,
'I had better go back to Dundalk!'

There was a Young Person of Ayr,
Whose head was remarkably square:
On the top, in fine weather, she wore a gold feather;
Which dazzled the people of Ayr.

There was an Old Person of Skye,
Who waltz'd with a Bluebottle fly:
They buzz'd a sweet tune, to the light of the moon,
And entranced all the people of Skye.

There was an Old Man of Dumblane,
Who greatly resembled a crane;
But they said,—'Is it wrong, since your legs are so long,
To request you won't stay in Dumblane?'

There was an Old Person of Hyde,
Who walked by the shore with his bride,
Till a Crab who came near, fill'd their bosoms with fear,
And they said, 'Would we'd never left Hyde!'

There was an Old Person of Rimini,
Who said, 'Gracious! Goodness! O Gimini!'
When they said, 'Please be still!' she ran down a hill,
And was never more heard of at Rimini.

There was an Old Man in a tree,
Whose whiskers were lovely to see;
But the birds of the air, pluck'd them perfectly bare,
To make themselves nests in that tree.

There was a Young Lady of Corsica,
Who purchased a little brown saucy-cur;
Which she fed upon ham, and hot raspberry jam,
That expensive Young Lady of Corsica.

There was an Old Person of Bray,
Who sang through the whole of the day
To his ducks and his pigs, whom he fed upon figs,
That valuable Person of Bray.

There was an Old Person of Sestri,
Who sate himself down in the vestry,
When they said 'You are wrong!'—he merely said 'Bong!'
That repulsive Old Person of Sestri.

There was an Old Person of Bude,
Whose deportment was vicious and crude;
He wore a large ruff, of pale straw-coloured stuff,
Which perplexed all the people of Bude.

There was an Old Person of Bow,
Whom nobody happened to know;
So they gave him some soap, and said coldly, 'We hope
You will go back directly to Bow!'

There was a Young Lady of Greenwich,
Whose garments were border'd with Spinach;
But a large spotty Calf, bit her shawl quite in half,
Which alarmed that Young Lady of Greenwich.

There was an Old Person of Brigg,
Who purchased no end of a wig;
So that only his nose, and the end of his toes,
Could be seen when he walked about Brigg.

There was an Old Person of Crowle,
Who lived in the nest of an owl;
When they screamed in the nest, he screamed out
    with the rest,
That depressing Old Person of Crowle.

There was an Old Person in gray,
Whose feelings were tinged with dismay;
She purchased two parrots, and fed them with carrots,
Which pleased that Old Person in gray.

There was an Old Person of Blythe,
Who cut up his meat with a scythe;
When they said, 'Well! I never!'—he cried,
   'Scythes for ever!'
That lively Old Person of Blythe.

There was an Old Person of Ealing,
Who was wholly devoid of good feeling;
He drove a small gig, with three Owls and a Pig,
Which distressed all the people of Ealing.

There was an Old Person of Ickley,
Who could not abide to ride quickly,
He rode to Karnak, on a tortoise's back,
That moony Old Person of Ickley.

There was an Old Man of Ancona,
Who found a small dog with no owner,
Which he took up and down, all the streets of the town;
That anxious Old Man of Ancona.

There was an Old Person of Grange,
Whose manners were scroobious and strange;
He sailed to St. Blubb, in a waterproof tub,
That aquatic Old Person of Grange.

There was an Old Person of Nice,
Whose associates were usually Geese.
They walked out together, in all sorts of weather,
That affable Person of Nice!

There was an Old Person of Deal
Who in walking, used only his heel;
When they said, 'Tell us why?'—he made no reply;
That mysterious Old Person of Deal.

There was an Old Man of Thermopylæ,
Who never did anything properly;
But they said, 'If you choose, to boil eggs in your shoes,
You shall never remain in Thermopylæ.'

There was an Old Person of Minety
Who purchased five hundred and ninety
Large apples and pears, which he threw unawares,
At the heads of the people of Minety.

There was an Old Man whose despair
Induced him to purchase a hare:
Whereon one fine day, he rode wholly away,
Which partly assuaged his despair.

There was an Old Person of Pinner,
As thin as a lath, if not thinner;
They dressed him in white, and roll'd him up tight,
That elastic Old Person of Pinner.

There was an Old Person of Bromley,
Whose ways were not cheerful or comely;
He sate in the dust, eating spiders and crust,
That unpleasing Old Person of Bromley.

There was an Old Man of Dunrose;
A parrot seized hold of his nose.
When he grew melancholy, they said, 'His name's Polly,'
Which soothed that Old Man of Dunrose.

There was an Old Man on the Border,
Who lived in the utmost disorder;
He danced with the cat, and made tea in his hat,
Which vexed all the folks on the Border.

There was an Old Man of Spithead,
Who opened the window, and said,—
'Fil-jomble, fil-jumble, fil-rumble-come-tumble!'
That doubtful Old Man of Spithead.

There was an Old Person of Sheen,

Whose expression was calm and serene;

He sate in the water, and drank bottled porter,

That placid Old Person of Sheen.

There was an Old Person of Florence,
Who held mutton chops in abhorrence;
He purchased a Bustard, and fried him in Mustard,
Which choked that Old Person of Florence.

There was an Old Person of Loo,
Who said, 'What on earth shall I do?'
When they said, 'Go away!'—she continued to stay,
That vexatious Old Person of Loo.

There was an Old Person of Pisa,
Whose daughters did nothing to please her;
She dressed them in gray, and banged them all day,
Round the walls of the city of Pisa.

There was an Old Man in a garden,
Who always begged every-one's pardon;
When they asked him, 'What for?'—he replied
    'You're a bore!
And I trust you'll go out of my garden.'

There was an Old Man of Thames Ditton,
Who called for something to sit on;
But they brought him a hat, and said—'Sit upon that,
You abruptious Old Man of Thames Ditton!'

There was an Old Man of Dee-side
Whose hat was exceedingly wide,
But he said 'Do not fail, if it happen to hail
To come under my hat at Dee-side!'

There was an Old Man at a Station,
Who made a promiscuous oration;
But they said, 'Take some snuff! You have talk'd
     quite enough
You afflicting Old Man at a Station!'

There was an Old Person of Shields,
Who frequented the valley and fields;
All the mice and the cats, and the snakes and the rats,
Followed after that Person of Shields.

There was a Young Person in pink,
Who called out for something to drink;
But they said, 'O my daughter, there's nothing but water!'
Which vexed that Young Person in pink.

There was a Young Person whose history,
Was always considered a mystery;
She sate in a ditch, although no one knew which,
And composed a small treatise on history.

There was an Old Person of Dutton,
Whose head was so small as a button:
So to make it look big, he purchased a wig,
And rapidly rushed about Dutton.

TWENTY-SIX NONSENSE RHYMES

The Absolutely Abstemious Ass,
who resided in a Barrel, and only lived on
Soda Water and Pickled Cucumbers.

The Bountiful Beetle,
who always carried a Green Umbrella when it didn't rain,
and left it at home when it did.

The Comfortable Confidential Cow,
who sate in her Red Morocco Arm Chair and
toasted her own Bread at the parlour Fire.

The Dolomphious Duck,
who caught Spotted Frogs for her dinner
with a Runcible Spoon.

The Enthusiastic Elephant,
who ferried himself across the water with the
Kitchen Poker and a New pair of Ear-rings.

The Fizzgiggious Fish,
who always walked about upon Stilts
because he had no legs.

The Goodnatured Grey Gull,
who carried the Old Owl, and his Crimson Carpet-bag,
across the river, because he could not swim.

The Hasty Higgeldipiggledy Hen,
who went to market in a Blue Bonnet and Shawl,
and bought a Fish for her Supper.

The Inventive Indian,
who caught a Remarkable Rabbit in a
Stupendous Silver Spoon.

The Judicious Jubilant Jay,
who did up her Back Hair every morning with a
 Wreath of Roses
Three feathers, and a Gold Pin.

The Kicking Kangaroo,
who wore a Pale Pink Muslin dress
with Blue spots.

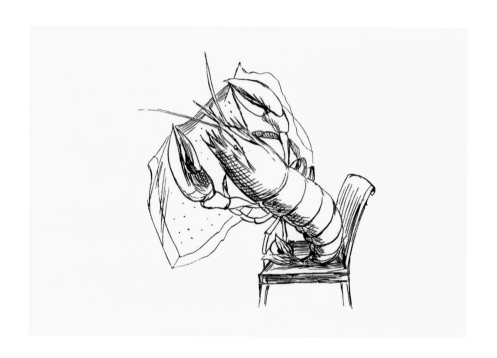

The Lively Learned Lobster,
who mended his own Clothes with
a Needle and Thread.

The Melodious Meritorious Mouse,
who played a merry minuet on the
Piano-forte.

The Nutritious Newt,
who purchased a Round Plum-pudding
for his grand-daughter.

The Obsequious Ornamental Ostrich,
who wore Boots to keep his
feet quite dry.

The Perpendicular Purple Polly,
who read the Newspaper and ate Parsnip Pie
with his Spectacles.

The Queer Querulous Quail,
who smoked a Pipe of tobacco on the top of
a Tin Tea-kettle.

The Rural Runcible Raven,
who wore a White Wig and flew away
with the Carpet Broom.

The Scroobious Snake,
who always wore a Hat on his Head, for
fear he should bite anybody.

The Tumultuous Tom-tommy Tortoise,
who beat a Drum all day long in the
middle of the wilderness.

The Umbrageous Umbrella-maker,
whose Face nobody ever saw, because it was
always covered by his Umbrella.

The Visibly Vicious Vulture,
who wrote some Verses to a Veal-cutlet in a
Volume bound in Vellum.

The Worrying Whizzing Wasp,
who stood on a Table, and played sweetly on a
Flute with a Morning Cap.

The Excellent Double-extra XX
imbibing King Xerxes, who lived a
long while ago.

The Yonghy-Bonghy-Bo,
whose Head was ever so much bigger than his
Body, and whose Hat was rather small.

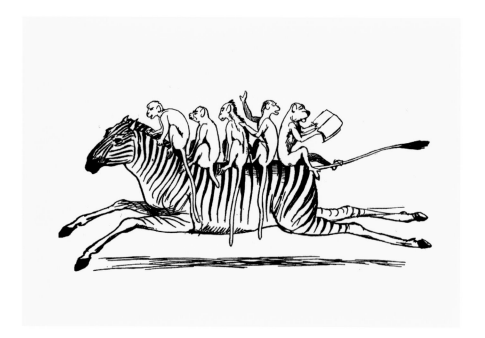

The Zigzag Zealous Zebra,
who carried five Monkeys on his back all
the way to Jellibolee.

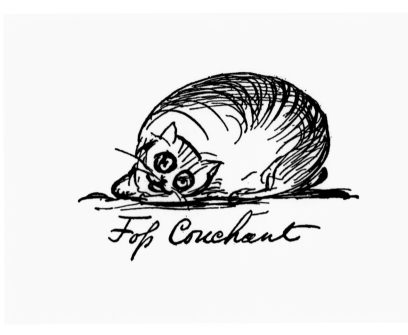

Foss Couchant

THE HERALDIC BLAZON
OF FOSS THE CAT

Foss, a untin.

Foss
rampant

Fob dansant

Feb, regardant

Joh Pprpr.

Foss, Passant